Soul Gardening

Jeremy Naydler

Godstow Press

First published 2006 by
Godstow Press
60 Godstow Road
Oxford OX2 8NY
Tel. 01865 556215

www.godstowpress.co.uk

Copyright © 2005 Jeremy Naydler

ISBN 0-9547367-3-7

All rights reserved.
No part of this book may be
reproduced in any form without the
prior permission of the publisher.

Illustrations by Jeremy Naydler
Typeset by Alacrity, Banwell Castle
Cover design by Joanna Migdal and George White,
in conjunction with DL Designs

Printed by Athenæum Press Ltd., Gateshead

About the Author

Jeremy Naydler has worked as a gardener for many years, serving his apprenticeship in York in the 1970s and subsequently working in various gardens in the leafy Victorian suburbs of north Oxford. The poems gathered together in this volume stem from his experience of gardening as a labour that 'seems ever to bend itself back toward soul'. For him, all gardening is soul work, and these poems live at the interface of soul and garden, where inner experience finds itself reflected in outer reality, and where outer reality speaks of deep, often deeply challenging, inner experience. Ultimately, the work of the gardener involves not only ensouling the garden but also gardening the soul.

As an author, Jeremy is best known for his in-depth researches into the religious life of the ancient Egyptians: *Temple of the Cosmos* (1996) and *Shamanic Wisdom in the Pyramid Texts* (2005). He is also author of *How Caterpillars Acquire Wings*, and *Goethe on Science* and his articles and reviews have been published in a variety of journals including *Resurgence*, *The Ecologist* and *Caduceus*. As well as being a gardener and a writer, Jeremy holds a doctorate in theology and religious studies and has for many years worked in adult education, lecturing at the universities of Oxford, Reading and Southampton on the history of philosophy and on ancient Egyptian religion.

CONTENTS

Introduction v

Part One: The Soul of the Garden

The Gardener's Hand	3
Lines in Response to Vita Sackville-West's Sissinghurst	5
Beatitude	6
The First and Last Thing	7
Winter Dialogue	10
The Plants Who Teach Me All I Know	11
The World That I This Afternoon Destroyed	12

Part Two: Of Small Creatures

Prologue	16
The Deer	18
Grass	21
To the Gentle Worm	22
Foxglove	24
To the Nettle	25
The Spider	27
Crocus	28
To the Woodlouse	29

Busy Bee	30
The Ecstasy of the Bee	30
The Nettle in the Basil Pot	32
The Little Grub	34

Part Three: The Songs of Slug

Prologue	38
Lament	43
'I sing of slug...'	44
'Slug, How I would be rid of you!'	45
'I am slug...'	46
'O slug I see in you...'	48
Pity Slug, his Ugliness Forgive	50

Part Four: Mottoes and Proverbs

Part Five: The Garden of the Soul

I The Gardener	58
The Priesthood	60
When Day on Day	61
The Greenhouse	62
In Deepest Yin	64
When By Moonlight	65
Gardener's Song 1	67
Gardener's Song 2	68

INTRODUCTION

The poems gathered together in this volume were written over a period of more than twenty years. During this time I have worked in many different gardens, finding this the form of employment closest to my idea of paradise. For most of my adult life, I have spent every afternoon in one garden or another. Mornings I always keep reserved for labours of a different kind: intellectual and mostly pursued indoors. But my afternoons have belonged to the gardens, and that is when I let go of the intellectual mode and embrace simplicity.

People sometimes say to me that gardening is a good time for thinking. But I have never found it so. My mind is usually blissfully empty when I'm gardening. Every now and then, however, into this empty mind have come one or two lines of a poem, as if from another level of the activity of gardening, to which I should attend. Often, of course, I do not attend. But when I have attended, and have allowed the lines to work on me while weeding or pruning, or while making a bonfire or sitting in a greenhouse on a rainy afternoon, then a poem might eventually emerge.

I am used to referring to these poems as my 'garden poems', partly to distinguish them from my mostly completely unpublishable 'other poems', and partly because they belong to the gardens and to that part of my life which I have given to being a gardener. But I have gradually come to see that they are as much 'soul poems' as garden poems. The labour of gardening seems ever to bend itself back toward soul, and the more so the longer we do it.

What I have come to realise is that although gardening may seem superficially to be mostly rather humdrum work, there is another level to it that one does not find very often acknowledged. And I do not mean the aesthetic level. This of course is important, and all good gardeners are aware that gardening is as much an art form as sculpting or making music. But beyond aesthetic sensitivity there is another kind of sensitivity which is not so easy to put into words. It can give us the experience that the garden is not simply 'out there' but is just as much an internal reality. And this internal reality is OUR internal reality. It is the soul. Soul and garden are interfused.

All gardening is soul-work, and one is not truly gardening if one separates the two. These poems were born from the interface of soul and garden, where inner experience finds itself reflected in outer reality, and where outer reality speaks of deep, often deeply challenging, inner experience. For this reason I dedicate these poems to all those gardeners who would know that, in truth, the work of the gardener involves not only ensouling the garden but also gardening the soul.

September 2005

PART ONE

THE SOUL OF THE GARDEN

THE GARDENER'S HAND

Gentle is the gardener's hand
that sows the seed
that calls the plant
from stars above:
within his heart
the garden's soul
does find a voice,
does gain an eye:
through him the garden
comes to life,
becomes a whole,
and yearns to know
its heart of joy.
The gardener's hand
does hold the seed
in which the spirit
of the garden stirs.
O gentle is the hand
that, opening,
lets the spirit grow.

LINES IN RESPONSE TO VITA SACKVILLE-WEST'S SISSINGHURST

*'Profusion, even extravagance and exuberance,
within the confines of the utmost linear severity.'*
                    V.S.W. on Sissinghurst

I've had enough of gardens where
what's wild and rough
is smoothed and squeezed
into forms that please
the controlling mind.

The time is here
to put away our fear
of what's exuberant:
Throw out the plan,
the ordered line,
and the clipped box hedge!

The place of the garden
is on the edge
where what's below
meets what's above.

A garden is a bird set free,
a soaring dove:
a wilderness
fostered by human love.

BEATITUDE

Blessed are the gardeners
who see a heaven filled with stars
where the daisies lie in showers
and a golden sun
in every dandelion;
who in the pure light passing
through the white cherry flowers
feel the breath of angels
blow through the hours;
who, as the leaves of spring unfold,
know that through the garden
runs the axis of the world.

THE FIRST AND LAST THING

I settle easy in my toil
seeding spirits in the soil,
I lure them down,
I draw them through,
and in the earth
they chew on roots
of starlight made
and lay their thoughts in balances,
to be weighed between the earth and sky.
They never need to question why,
for every thing they think,
they know.

And in the spray
on misty days
more spirits do I sow –
scattering them upon the vapours
where they melt
like warming flakes of snow,
and move as if the fabric of their images
was of living dreams composed,
infusing from within
the tender life of leaf and stem.

And then to radiant air I turn:
I love to feel the spirits dance
the atmosphere around the plants,
blushing petals with their joy,
weaving sunbeams to enchant
the sacred sweet environment,
for they are never far away
in light and shade, by night and day,
where flower meets air
and seed breathes fire.

And there, inside the seed,
I delve as far as mind can see,
to glimpse a world of mystery
so deep, it is beyond all place,
both within and outside space:
where matter melts and turns to fire
there daimons streak in flames of desire.

Oh do not ask me where they are:
I lure them down,
I draw them through,
and they're so thin they disappear
into the elements so near,
yet are so wide they fill our view.

They are the life, the energy,
the atmosphere and mood we share
and we must feed them
with our care.

The first and last thing
that the gardener knows is –
love alone green innocence grows.
And all the colours of delight,
the wondrous odours of the night,
each burgeoning form – root, stem and flower –
the plenitude that tumbles through the hours,
would turn to deserts of despair
if spirits were not harboured there.

WINTER DIALOGUE

'My plants, my friends, where are you now?
You have gone, gone, withered and gone.
And a dreadful stillness deadens the air –
your life and beauty are no longer there.'

'We have made our home in another place,
flown so deep in our retreat
we've abandoned form, abandoned space,
slipped through the world and into the night,
far away and out of sight.
Yet we're as close as the breath of your sigh,
close as the pupil of your inner eye.'

'My plants, my friends, I see you now:
You have come, invisibly you have come,
and a wondrous stillness enlivens the air –
your life and beauty are everywhere.'

THE PLANTS WHO TEACH ME
ALL I KNOW

The plants, who teach me all I know,
have shown me it is part of life
to be frozen and formless
in the dark below.

Dying, the thing that we most dread,
each year they readily embrace:
I bow to them, my friends the plants,
who shed their forms with such good grace.

They give themselves to winter's night,
and then, when all's completely lost,
from dark and cold they rise again
and strive, strive, *strive* for the light.

THE WORLD THAT I THIS AFTERNOON DESTROYED

The world that I this afternoon destroyed
for a moment on my conscience hung
while I did hesitate –

this world, whose canopy of sky I'd raised,
and into distant places flung,
awoke from dead stone's weight,

its caves of root and dust to light exposed
and all the lives that to them clung
upon my will did wait

while I, more god than man, their souls surveyed:
my eye was like the searing sun
no creature could escape.

Thus I the god did ape,
while deep within me dark doubts spun
a moral web my godlike power deposed

as I did contemplate
how often human lives are stung
by gods whose hands a conscience never stayed

as they prescribe each fate
and we in fortune's pot are swung,
raised up and blessed, or cursed, cast down and
                                        crazed.

How could I see my power like theirs deployed
on innocents the earth has sung
to life, inebriate?

And so I stood, by troubled thoughts waylaid,
and resolution would not come,
until one thought did shake

my mind, and this all my reflections closed:
each world to greater worlds belongs
and none is separate

– no thing lives separate
from the whole, through which life runs
as breath by which a thousand flutes are played,

the one song to create,
and I, a singer of this song,
whose harmony demands lives be destroyed

that others generate,
and I... to do right, must do wrong.
Thus my unquiet conscience was allayed.

For worlds are swept away to be remade
and all that's done will be undone
that life proliferate;

as seeds that germinate
must die in order to become,
so by death's dumb destructions is life praised.

PART TWO

OF SMALL CREATURES

PROLOGUE

Before the magnificent plants that grow in the gardens – the peonies, roses, and delphiniums and so many others – I stand in awe. They are the aristocracy of the plant world, like the lions and the elephants of the animal world. I bow to them, but I have never felt I could write a poem that could possibly do them justice.

I feel differently towards the more humble creatures with which I have daily passing encounters. They bring me up against the wild strangeness of the natural world in a different way, in a more informal way perhaps. The frequency of the daily encounters can cast a veil of familiarity that masks their strangeness, but I always meet it if I can stop myself in the midstream of my intentions and take time to relate to them. It is an 'otherness' that demands that I step outside the parameters of my purely subjective concerns.

Gardening is about relationship, and for me it has always entailed finding a bond of commonality between myself and the 'otherness' of the non-human creatures that I meet through the day.

Although so utterly different from me, they nevertheless mirror back to me soul-qualities that I recognise. The 'others' constitute a kind of soul-environment. Just as a dream presents us with persons and environments that are both familiar and unfamiliar, both within us and yet seemingly autonomous, living in a life-stream that is independent of our day-consciousness, so the world of plants and small creatures mirrors back to us a soul-environment to which we belong, even though it is not 'our own'. While it is not our own, it is nevertheless part of the greater soul-world in which we, along with all living creatures, share.

If gardening were to be thought of as a spiritual path, this perhaps would be one reason why: it requires of us that we step outside our own self-referential and circumscribed 'human' nature in order to connect with a greater nature, the one world that we share with all other creatures, no matter how different from us they may seem.

THE DEER

Once I saw a nimble deer
after a night of storm
come through my fence,
through flowers and mist,
to drink from my pool at dawn.
A stranger from another world
– all grace and sensitivity –
it stood quivering on my lawn.

A familiar voice admonished me
in words I have come to dread:
'This deer will eat your precious plants

and trample your flowerbeds.
Don't stand and stare –
be vigilant,
and act from common sense.
If you were a proper gardener
you'd drive it off
and then repair the fence!'

From the upper window
where I stood,
I saw how softly on the grass
the gentle creature trod,

as if the bluebells in the nearby wood
had trained it to tread
upon the ground
as one would tread
the unearthly blue sky overhead,
without crushing so much as a whisp of cloud.

How could I drive it away?
I wanted rather to honour its stay,
by light of sun or moon –
this wandering guest
from the wilderness
who would be gone too soon.

And so I watched
as the mild deer stopped
and mildly drank from my pond,
bestowing on my garden
all the blessing of the wild.

Now time has passed and years gone by
since the deer first used to come:
my plants overflow, more precious than gold,
but my garden fences I still dare
to leave in a state of ill-repair.

And from where my fence is broken
an unseen deerpath runs
that leads to a hidden woodland dell,
where windflowers blow and nettles grow,
where brambles stretch and ferns unfurl
and timid little creatures dwell,
and bluebells turning blue.

Into this woodland garden
the wild deer often stray,
and there by light of sun or moon
I too would find my way.

GRASS

Grass is grass: it has no other name
than grass – because it's all the same...
except for one majestic month in June
when grass throws off its humbleness,
ascends beyond the mute green blade
and blooms: and then
each blade, each stem,
shakes out a little diadem of flowers:
grass then no longer is just grass
but the joy of angels
as they stop and pass.

TO THE GENTLE WORM

Gentle worm within the soil
invisible to us you toil;
somewhere down beneath our feet,
the earthy roots and grubs you greet.
Your form with mildness is imbued –
to other creatures you are food,
and yet none other would you harm
in anger, hunger or alarm.

Your humble throat with earth you fill,
and from your mouth no sound does spill:
you do not growl nor do you roar,
you do not have sharp tooth or claw,
nor fearsome horn nor poison fang.

When from the earth each creature sprang,
you stayed within your mother's womb,
unwilling to depart so soon,
swimming through the soil, your sea,
underneath the apple tree,
hidden from fierce angels' sight,
innocent of wrong and right.

And in your world, where all is dark,
where no cat howls nor dog does bark,
hour on hour you toil away
and never know the light of day.

Do you ever laugh or weep?
Do you dream or fall asleep?
To whom is it your life belongs?
Your flesh feeds the blackbird's song,
and everything that you excrete
nourishes the plants we eat.

The garden would, without you, die,
the blackbird lose its strength to fly,
the earth would sour and roots would rot,
deserts grow where you are not.

To you in gratitude we bend
for on you do our lives depend.

FOXGLOVE

Freckled foxglove,
you grow between worlds,
friend both of bees and elves –
liminal plant
you live on the edge
breathing sunlight and mist,
fine ether and air.
Child of the hedgerow
and roadside drift,
child of poetry and myth,
child of this world
and worlds unseen,
you grow where you want,
half wild, half tame,
half here, half there,
ever in between.

TO THE NETTLE

Dear nettle, if you should lose your sting,
or have it prised from you by some dark science,
how could I love you then as I do now?
And if your tiny, tumbling flowers be made to swell
or tint with colour brash or heady scent,
you would to me your beauty then have lost
by this and all such false improvement.

Stay wild, my friend, and fierce upon my borders:
stand guard where realm of artifice does end
and spirits imperceptible to sense
live poised upon the margins of disorder.
The grub that grazes on your leaf defend,
its predators of ignorance and wrath deflect,
and all the denizens of the wild protect.

THE SPIDER

Each day when I walk through my gate –
the silver spider's web I break.
Oh little spider, are you there?
– your threads, so fine, are in my hair.

The spinner, though, I never see,
no doubt dismayed that it's caught me.
I am too big a prey for you –
I break your threads, not meaning to.

And you have laboured all night long
to catch a prey too big and strong.
Sometimes I wish I were a fly
to right the wrong, but I ask why

you weave webs in the very place
where they get tangled in my face.
Oh please don't weave them there again:
you should be catching flies, not men.

CROCUS

She said she held the crocus in disdain
for foolishly opening to the sun
in the season of freezing winds and rain.
'It is so ineffectual' – she went on:
'Its stem is weak, it cannot stay erect,
its petals are too bright and much too large!
Now *snowdrops* are a plant I *can* respect:
the sensible snowdrop – well camouflaged,
and holds its head the right way round.
It is no idiotic optimist
but understands its flowers must face the ground.
Unlike crocus, it is a realist.'
    But something in me at her words did smart:
for crocus has such openness of heart.

TO THE WOODLOUSE

Dear humble woodlouse,
always so calm,
your pace never quickens
as you trundle along.

How many times
has your world been broken
and shattered
and thrown upside down?

But while you may tumble,
and the ground beneath you crumble,
you carry on unflappable,
forever affable.

Dear woodlouse
please teach me,
when my world is shaken,
and my sky become starless,
how I may, like you,
keep trundling on regardless.

BUSY BEE

Busy bee, buzz in my ear –
the nectar that you look for there
you will not find:
my ear is far too unrefined.
It has no scent, nor petals rare,
no pistil sweet nor stamen there –
for bees it is an empty bowl:
its honey hides within my soul.

THE ECSTASY OF THE BEE

Oh flower, my heart,
I touch your wings
with my humming furs:
see how I move
while you are grounded!
I feed on your joy
and take it
to the farthest reaches
of your imagination.

Your soul is mine,
my tongue is suffused,
intoxicated with your honey.
How could I bear
to part from you, my life?
I browse and hum
to the secret rhythms of your scent,
see how I am glorified in you!
how I ravish you:
I gorge myself on your dreaming.

Oh flower,
look how I destroy your symmetry!
How clumsy is this my ecstasy
that loosens your petals
to the insatiate worm.

Oh flower,
though you fear my coming,
your delight is my feeding,
for I set your soul free
to fly through the air.

THE NETTLE IN THE BASIL POT

It was the nettle in the basil pot
that caught me out again.
I was reaching for those fragrant leaves
and was met by stinging pain.

If only I'd remembered
I would have taken care
to notice that, like yesterday,
the nettle was still there.

It was growing wild and wily
in the greenhouse warm,
having come in from the cold outside,
blown in by the storm:

into the basil pot it leapt,
a refugee from the frost;
I should have known the basil leaves
were no longer free of cost.

Like a lover, stung by fortune
yet goaded by desire,
I learn my lessons badly
and burn my fingers in the fire.

Each day I go to the greenhouse
and see the basil pot
but forget about the nettle,
then forget that I forgot.

Sweet nettle, sting me one more time
to make me more aware,
so when next I pick the basil
I remember to take more care.

THE LITTLE GRUB

The little grub within the earth
felt so sad and low;
'In this mud, what is of worth?
Of heaven, what do I know?'

A butterfly was passing by
and hearing grub's lament
said: 'Little grubs that wish to fly
need wings for their ascent.'

'I have no wings', said little grub,
'and wings I cannot grow.
I just flounder in the mud:
no higher can I go,'

The winged one settled on the ground,
and to the grub she said:
'Nourishment for wings is found
in this your earthy bed.

'Don't you despair, now, little grub,
for I was once like you.
Through all the trials of the mud
these wings I slowly grew.'

The grub curled up beneath a stone,
and like a stone became.
Deep depressed and all alone
wished never to wake again.

But now it dreamed a wondrous dream
of stars and moon and sun;
and things that it had never seen,
and never before done.

A long time passed. Then grub awoke
and felt so free of care
it wriggled out from its abode
and wriggled more in sheer delight

and wriggling so, felt suddenly light:
grub rose up in the air!

'Was I a grub?' the Winged One said
'with a little grub-like soul?
In truth I never was a grub.
But living in my earthy bed
through all my pain and woe,
it was not grub that wept and bled
but I – a Winged One,

wingless in the mud,
yet only in the mud
could these my wings
begin to grow.'

PART THREE

THE SONGS OF SLUG

PROLOGUE

Of all the sounds of the night, there is one that I shall always remember. It is a sound that causes me to shudder in repulsion even as I think of it now. I first heard it one evening when I stood among my vegetables, trying to identify what on earth it was. Then the full horror of its meaning dawned on me: it was the sound of a thousand slugs chomping through my lettuces, my brussels sprouts and my cabbages, demolishing my beetroot, spinach and tender young beans.

From that night on, and for the following three years, I waged ceaseless war on the slugs. Night after night I sallied forth, picking them off my plants one by one, and dropping them in jars of deadly salted water. In the summer months, you would find me out at midnight among my vegetables, filling up one jar after another with my hated foes, who soon dissolved into a foul-smelling goo.

How many did I kill? At first I kept a record. It was often a hundred, sometimes a hundred and fifty, even two hundred, each night. For three summers I exhausted myself in this fruitless war, for no matter how many I killed, there were always more, appearing as if from the depths of a dark and malevolent underworld.

I tried many different methods. I became an expert in the various means of dispatching slugs, but I found none to be as effective as picking them off by hand. Yet even this method, despite the many thousands of slugs I killed, seemed to do no more than stem the tide for a few days, a week at the most. And then I was back again at the beginning, facing another onslaught.

One day, in the midst of this Mahabharata, an incident occurred that was to have a powerful impact on my campaign. A friend of mine, someone who I regard as far more spiritually advanced than I could ever hope to become in this lifetime, caused me great amusement when she found a snail on the path and, taking pity on it, carefully set it down in a shady place under a shrub. 'I can tell you are not a gardener!' I said. But the act stayed with me and worked on me, worked into me, worked into my conscience.

I had already by this time begun to research my enemies. I had made several visits to the library, curious to find out what I could about snails and slugs. I learnt of their primeval origins, about their lifestyles and habits, and how certain slugs reproduce dangling from a single thread of mucus in the air. I learnt also of how these blind creatures are able to seek out their victims, and how their myriad teeth rip and tear them apart. My fascination began to overcome my repulsion. For the first time in my life, I got to know and recognise different species of slug and snail and, almost despite myself, I came to see them as beautiful. And seeing them as beautiful, I began to feel a new appreciation for them.

Goaded by a sense of shame on the one hand, and feeling a growing fondness for these creatures on the other, I at last declared an amnesty. I decided I would not attack them during daylight hours. But I still maintained my ferocious assaults on them by night. But soon the amnesty extended to Sunday nights, and then to more and more nights as I felt less and less able to pursue my war against them. For whatever repulsion that I felt towards them, it was far less than the repulsion that I now felt towards my own action of slaughtering them.

It was during this time of the winding down of the Slug Wars that I began to write these slug poems. And in so doing I made an astonishing discovery: the slug problem was clearly becoming less serious. Not only was I no longer haunted by them, but it seemed that their attacks on my plants were subsiding. As the initial truce turned into a lasting peace, it also assumed the character of a kind of friendship. I understood that all I needed to do for my vegetables was to take more care in what I grew and where and how I grew it, and the slugs and I could live with each other in mutual amity and respect.

But more than that, I realised the extent to which the battles I had been fighting were not simply against an outer enemy. I began to see the Slug Wars as campaigns against something in myself that these lowly creatures represented, and my murderous nightly vigils only showed me how in order to rid myself of their grotesque presence, I had myself become grotesque. All I could do now was to thank the slugs for holding a mirror to a part of myself of which I had not previously been conscious, and bow in reverence to that within their nature which now seemed to me not only beautiful but holy.

SIX SONGS OF SLUG

1

LAMENT

Within the earth where worm and woodlouse go
in utter vulnerability I grow –
and there in secret crevices it sleeps:
beside my tender spreading roots it keeps
its silent refuge from the warming sun
toward which I in all my longing turn.
Oh how I would speed from where it slouches
to the free space that my tendril touches.
But each night it stirs and creeps up my stem
and, helpless, I must surrender again:
my sap, my flesh, my fragile life it reaps,
and away from me my energy seeps –
    every part of me for its enjoying,
    its solitary love my life destroying.

2

I sing of slug
and his old sea soul:
he comes up from the deep,
from the damp and the dark;
he comes up slow
and out of sight,
and his primeval soul
is hungry for beautiful things,
for tender, vulnerable, growing things,
and he would devour them all
in secret delight.
Yes, all the gentle plants
that grow by day
would slug devour by night.

I sing of slug,
half-blind, unloved,
unloving ugly thing,
whose passionless blood
does dread the heat
and knows no pulse,
no beat, no rhythm.

Slug loves nothing
and gives to none,
cowers under the open sky
and crawls away from the sun.
O slug in me, I sing of you.

3

Slug, How I would be rid of you!
I would drown you in beer,
pour salt on your path,
and stamp on you in my futile wrath,
set frogs to gobble your young,
bring in hedgehogs and ducks;
I would myself a duck become
to snuffle you up
as you my plants have done.
How dare you live
on things so dear to me?
I wage war against you
for you are my inveterate enemy!

Yet closer to me than I dare to think,
I find you in that part of me
from which I shrink.

4

I am slug.
I have no eyes.
I cannot speak.
I like to eat
and be inert.
But there is more to me
than seems at first.

Lift a stone
and I am there.
Raise a log:
I am underneath.

To know my secret
watch me creep
like a soft grey tongue
oozing saliva
upon the dirt.
Then watch me copulating in the air:
with my mate I dangle there
for hour on hour,

caduceus-like,
no longer in my element.
I procreate part dove, part grub,
part snake.
Silently entwined
we speak our love.

I am slug.
Where there is life
there also am I,
God's humble shadow,
too low to be a demon,
I crawl up from behind the rock,
I hang upon the tree.
Though I seem foul,
there is nothing in the world
more beautiful than me.

5

O slug I see in you
a tongue incapable of speech
slipping soundlessly
across the earth.
In you God lives an alien to Himself
and therefore true.
You are the living Word asleep,
the rejected one
that feeds on dung –
your home the compost heap.

You are the deadly dewdrop on the vine,
the pearl of beauty thrown to swine,
and we are Judas, the pharisee,
the raging crowd that did not know you,
because we thought you were our enemy.

You are the spectre and the clown:
when things are up you bring them down.
In you God sings His silent song of death:
mocking pride of living forms
by making you make them bereft.

Though I've despised you
now I honour give:
Your destructiveness
I would not change,
for where there's loveliness
there you must live.
Your ugliness
is beauty self-estranged.

You are the slaughterer in life's dance:
through you God greets again the plants
so lately sprung from His domain:
a loss on earth is heaven's gain.

O slug, I cannot kill you.
And God, it seems, would not redeem you,
give you hope of wings, or flight.
You are merely and forever grub.
Your poverty will not be raised
to some false wealth.
O slug, I bow to you
in your dread holiness,
the alien within myself.

6

PITY SLUG, HIS UGLINESS FORGIVE

God made slug in likeness of a moving tongue:
dumb mouthless instrument of speech made flesh,
slug oozes slime, hides away from the sun
– in the dank and dark feels happiest,
To lovely things slug ever poses threat
– in dark of night he preys on loveliness
haunting joyful life with spectre of death,
taunting beauty with his ugliness.
And yet for beauty slug in secret yearns,
and in his wretchedness slug longs to die,
and dreams that he becomes a grub that turns
from ugly creeping thing to butterfly.
    So pity slug, his ugliness forgive:
        for in his heart a butterfly does live.

PART FOUR

MOTTOES AND PROVERBS

MOTTOES AND PROVERBS

1

The horror of plants:
to be eaten by slugs.
The disgust of plants:
to be sprayed against bugs.

The rapture of plants:
leaves wetted by rain.
The laughter of plants:
their Latin names.

2

Motto of the hoary weed:
Better to lose a leaf or two
than be pulled up by the root.

3

Motto of the hoary gardener:
Live as if you will die tomorrow,
garden as if you will live forever.

4

An optimistic proverb:
the worst weeds
make the best spring salads.

5

A pessimistic proverb:
it's a foolish gardener
who suppresses convolvulus
by planting ground elder.

6

After Blake:

the cut worm forgives
the gardener's spade;
the rose murmurs thanks
to the pruning blade.

7

An aroma of fine perfume in the air:
bonfire smoke in the gardener's hair.

8

What is the gardener's role?
It is to care for the garden's soul.
But what about the gardener's soul?
Well that of course is the garden's role.

9

The swallowed seed thanks the bird.

10

The buddleia speaks:
If you would grow stronger,
let yourself be cut down.

11

Pity the eye that sees only weeds.

12

The wisdom of the worm:
the harder your path through the earth,
the softer you must become.

PART FIVE

THE GARDEN OF THE SOUL

I THE GARDENER

I the gardener, planter out of roots,
midwife to ten thousand shoots,
dibber of bulbs, sower of seeds,
dreamer of great deeds, faithful servant
of the angel of this place,
this earth, this garden, celebrate.

The gardener's goal is to make whole,
to till the soil and swale the tilth,
to sow and grow and tend what's frail,
to foil the gale and heal through toil,
to forge a work of art.
But gardeners, if you would be whole,
you must be split apart.

I the gardener, rooter out of plants,
trimmer of stalks, scourge of weeds,
aesthete of wrath, demon servant
of the angel of this place,
I the garden do destroy
in order to create.

The gardener's art's to split apart,
shake earth from root, part clod from clod,
rip plant from sod, cut back and dock,
hack, rake and stake:
to grow you must fragment.
And gardeners, if you would be whole,
then first you must be rent.

I the gardener, garden am:
the plants about me are my selves,
my soul the soil that my spade delves,
my heart the yielding earth I till,
where my knife cuts, my blood I spill,
and my desire the seed I sow,
my deeds from love and pain I grow,
every sweet and poison thing
that is without and is within.

THE PRIESTHOOD

There is no temple less presuming
than this living temple here:
this garden that I love and live in,
priest and servant to the presence
that resides within its atmosphere.

I know no occupation,
none holier than this,
this priesthood of the garden.
And I, by millipede
and gentle worm ordained,
do only wish to serve
the spirit that dwells here
through wind, through sun, through rain.

WHEN DAY ON DAY

When day on day the sun's by cloud obscured,
its light bedulled, no flash of joy transmits,
how sad the rose that radiant sun adores,
its light-filled petals languishing unlit.

And yet from day sagacious slugs retreat
to find beneath some stone a place to rest,
and toads prefer the shade of compost heaps
where, still and quiet, they contemplate best.

It's said that birds sing sweetest in the rain,
and wisdom's owl no mouse does catch till dark,
and though these sunless days seem such a bain,
for owls it's easier by night to hit the mark.

   No matter, then, if clouds disturb our mind:
   on cloudy days an inner sun we'll find.

THE GREENHOUSE

Wild winds and storm may blow
rain, freezing hail and snow,
and all the trees and shrubs assail,
shock little leaf-bound grubs,
stop snails in their tracks,
drive cats through flaps
and frogs to refuge in their cracks,
fly birds to nest
and foxes back to ground,
but I to the greenhouse have already sped
leaving mudtrails from the flowerbed,
my fork stuck in a compost mound.

With the tender plants I sit,
the flowerpots and the bamboo sticks,
and the packets of seed unsown,
gazing warmly through the glass
at the wetness of the grass
in the gathering gloom,
while on the panes the droplets spread
and drips come dropping on my head.

In this fragile place of calm –
where by grace of glass so thin
the fury of the wind's disarmed –
I find relent
from the restless storm's
driving, destructive intent;
for here a stillness resides,
my inner strife subsides,
and as the darkness descends
I with solitude make friends,
and contentment meet
in my greenhouse retreat.

IN DEEPEST YIN

In deepest yin, the world has slid,
slowed down to sleep within itself.
And what was strong, and what was firm,
is weak and limp, its colour seeped,
its form withdrawn, its residue
returning to the elements.
As ember buried under ash,
in densest dark the fire is hid
for which the out-spent soul does yearn.
So to the dark it must give in,
as does the plant, surrendering
sap, surge and seed back to the earth.
Then soul, like plant, may round time's curve
and strike from hidden fire.... *rebirth*.

WHEN BY MOONLIGHT

When by moonlight the tulips are still closed,
like chalices on their quivering stems,
containing promises not yet disclosed
in this tenuous light (not yet for them
the blackbird's summons to unfold; the wren
is silent still within its little nest);
when breath of everything is held, potent,
and – coiled and quiet – the moonlit world's at rest,
to you, protector of my inwardness
I turn, that you may help me to sustain
this same gesture, that in my waywardness
I may to this inner chalice remain
true, for I would my restless heart compose
and tend those things that the heart alone knows.

GARDENER'S SONG 1

In gardens of gold I live my days –
probably I'll never mend my ways.
Bright flowers the tapestry on which I bend,
it is my ease to tend the plants:
it is my happiness.

Through seasons round and round I weave:
I gyre and spire, I mow and weed.
And I feel blessed,
and murmur prayers of thankfulness
that this can seem
so close a life to Adam's dream.

GARDENER'S SONG 2

I sing the garden through the day,
by night the garden sings in me:
my dream at night the garden's joy,
by day it is the garden's dream
that fills my heart.

O trees and flowers, dream in my blood
your love of God, in sun, in rain;
blood of my life I give to you –
my love of God through you is sung.
I serve, and serving find
this life of mine and yours is one.

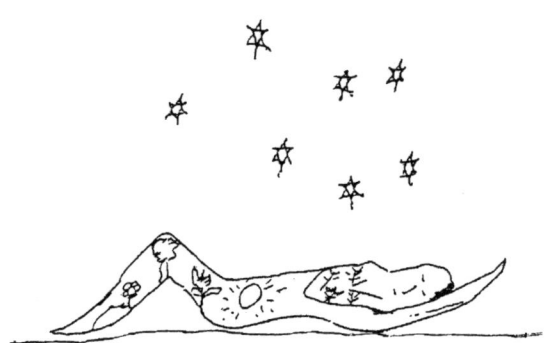

GODSTOW PRESS

Because philosophy arises from awe, a philosopher is bound in his way to be a lover of myths and poetic fables. Poets and philosophers are alike in being big with wonder.   St Thomas Aquinas

THE SONG OF ORPHEUS, the music that charms stones, wild animals and even the King of Hades, is the song of poets who have a sense of the divine at heart. For the forces of greed and evil to succeed, that song must be drowned out by noise.

What is today if not noisy? Not only in our society but within ourselves there is the clamour of many distractions. Just living life we forget ourselves and the song that we heard as children is heard but rarely if at all.

The aim of Godstow Press is to sing the Orphic song, through books of fiction, poetry and non-fiction, as well as through CDs. Besides publishing first editions we shall include on our list works which have been privately produced by writers and musicians who have thought, perhaps, that they sing alone.

Together, artist and audience, we shall form a choir.

If you would like to be on our mailing list, please get in touch with us.

Godstow Press
60 Godstow Road
Wolvercote
Oxford
OX2 8NY
UK

www.godstowpress.co.uk

info@godstowpress.co.uk

tel +44 (0)1865 556215